Year 3 Workbook

Published by Pearson Education Limited, 80 Strand, London, WC2R 0RL.
www.pearson.com/international-schools

Copies of official specifications for all Pearson Edexcel qualifications may be found on the website: https://qualifications.pearson.com

Text © Pearson Education Limited 2022
Project managed and edited by Just Content Limited
Designed and typeset by PDQ Digital Media Solutions Limited
Picture research by SPi
Original illustrations © Pearson Education Limited 2022
Cover design © Pearson Education Limited 2022

The right of Amber Field to be identified as the author of this work has been asserted by her in accordance with the Copyright, Designs and Patents Act 1988.

First published 2022

24 23
10 9 8 7 6 5

British Library Cataloguing in Publication Data
A catalogue record for this book is available from the British Library

ISBN 978 1 292 39676 7

Copyright notice
All rights reserved. No part of this publication may be reproduced in any form or by any means (including photocopying or storing it in any medium by electronic means and whether or not transiently or incidentally to some other use of this publication) without the written permission of the copyright owner, except in accordance with the provisions of the Copyright, Designs and Patents Act 1988 or under the terms of a licence issued by the Copyright Licensing Agency, 5th Floor, Shackleton House, 4 Battlebridge Lane, London, SE1 2HX (www.cla.co.uk). Applications for the copyright owner's written permission should be addressed to the publisher.

Printed in Great Britain by Bell and Bain Ltd, Glasgow

Acknowledgements
The publisher would like to thank the following for their kind permission to reproduce their photographs:

Cover acknowledgements
Shutterstock: Janna7/Shutterstock 1

Text acknowledgements
UNICEF UK Enterprises Ltd: The Rights Respecting Schools Award: UNICEF UK. Rights Respecting Schools Award, 28 Apr. 2021 104

Photos acknowledgements
123RF: makasanaphoto/123RF 48; Nilanjan Bhattacharya/123RF 43; apoplexia/123RF 43; tomas1111/123RF 52; Michael Rosskothen/123rf.com 67; Nikhil Patil/123RF 77; Jacek Chabraszewski/123RF 95; Johan Swanepoel/123rf.com 67; **Alamy Stock Photo:** ian woolcock/Alamy Stock Photo 48; Lee Hudson/Alamy Stock Photo 52; UWE ANSPACH/dpa picture alliance/Alamy Stock Photo 38; Kay & Karl Ammann/Avalon/Bruce Coleman Inc/Alamy Stock Photo 39; Monirul Alam/ZUMA Press, Inc./Alamy Stock Photo 40; **Shutterstock:** Matyas Rehak/Shutterstock 12; Susan Schmitz/Shutterstock 41; Learnmoreandmore/Shutterstock 48; vvoe/Shutterstock 52; Rich Carey/Shutterstock 54; Danita Delimont/Shutterstock 56; Alrandir/Shutterstock 63; Naronta/Shutterstock 66; Wutthichai Phosri/Shutterstock 66; sunsetman/Shutterstock 66; HollyHarry/Shutterstock 66; AirP72/Shutterstock 66; katatonia82/Shutterstock 122; Poznyakov/Shutterstock 122; rblfmr/Shutterstock 11; Sascha Preussner/Shutterstock 43; Hung Chung Chih/Shutterstock 43; Ian Rentoul/Shutterstock 52; Reflex Life/Shutterstock 52; Rudmer Zwerver/Shutterstock 52; Marcin Perkowski/Shutterstock 67; Mike Flippo/Shutterstock 67; Konstantnin/Shutterstock 67; 999119/Shutterstock 67; shama65/Shutterstock 94; Jazzmany/Shutterstock 113; 4 PM production/Shutterstock 64; Christian Musat/Shutterstock 67; **Getty Images:** Quarter Studios/iStock/Getty Images Plus/Getty Images 45; posteriori/istock/Getty Images 11; Jemal Countess/Getty Images 40; George Pachantouris/Getty Images 47; **Sian Bradfield:** Sian Bradfield/Pearson Education Australia Pty Ltd 95

All other images © Pearson Education

Contents

Social Justice	9
Peace and Conflict	27
Sustainable Development	41
Identity and Diversity	68
Globalisation and Interdependence	81
Human Rights	101
Power and Governance	117
Glossary	127

Welcome to Global Citizenship!

We hope you will find this book useful as you approach the exciting subject of Global Citizenship! This book will form a key part of your journey to becoming a Global Citizen. It will help you understand the wider world, your place in it, how you can engage with issues locally and globally and how you can enact positive change.

Objective
This is what you will know or be able to do by the end of the session.

We will learn
This is what you will be learning in the session.

Key vocabulary
These are important words to know.

Information
This is an introduction to the session.

Social Justice 23

Challenging injustice

Objective

SJE3.ID – Begin to recognise stereotypes, generalisations and assumptions and to understand that they can be harmful and inaccurate.

We will learn:
- the meaning of the words 'stereotype' and 'discrimination'
- how to recognise stereotypes, generalisations and assumptions
- to recognise that they can be harmful.

Key vocabulary

assumptions, discrimination, generalisations, stereotype

ⓘ Sometimes, people can have fixed ideas about another group of people and they think that group of people are all the same. For example, someone might think that all girls like pink. This is a stereotype. We need to recognise when we see a stereotype, know that they can be harmful and have some ideas about how to tackle them.

Introduction   5

This book provides a clear structure to your learning. Each unit is based around a Global Citizenship strand and clearly focuses on the mastery of key objectives. These objectives are set out at the start of each session, along with the opportunity to reflect on what you have learned at the end of each session in the unit.

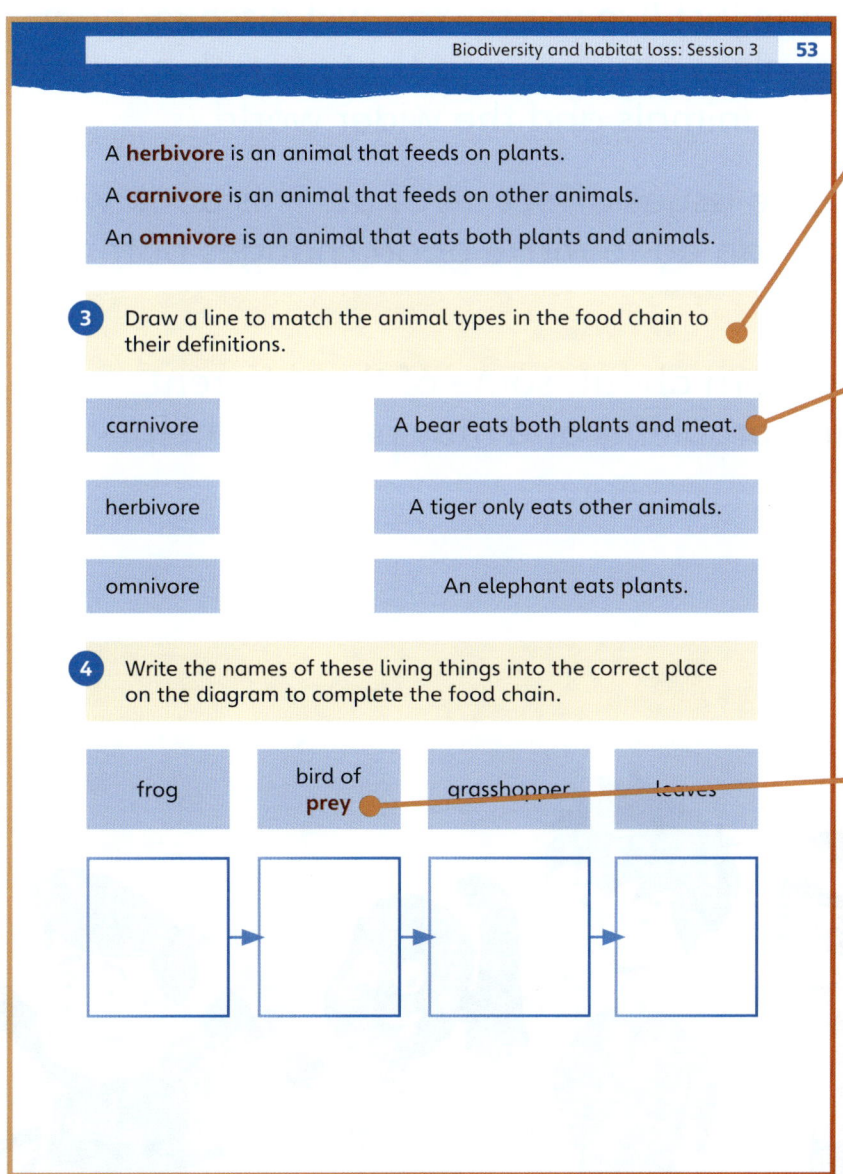

Instruction
Read this carefully to know what to do.

Activity
You might need to write or draw an answer, circle pictures or words, or tick or match answers.

Key vocabulary
Some tricky words are in **bold**. Find out what these mean in the Glossary at the back of the book.

You might have a question to think about or discuss with a Talk Partner or adult.

Meet the mascots!

Global Citizens!

We are all part of a Global Community – we are Global Citizens!

In this book you will meet lots of different people. Some may seem to be like you and some may seem to be different. However, everyone you meet will have something in common with you! Some may be from a part of the world you know, or from a city, town or village just like yours. You will discover how we are all part of a Global Community and that everything we do has effects on people, animals and the wider world.

You will find that the same issues affect all of us. This book will help you learn what you can do to make good changes both locally and globally.

You will also meet, and learn about, some of the different animals which are facing problems and may need our help.

The Giant Panda

Giant Pandas now only live in China and are very rare. People are trying to protect their homes from destruction. Protecting their homes also helps a lot of other animals and provides them with somewhere to live.

The Malayan Tapir

Malayan Tapirs are found in parts of South-East Asia. Young tapirs are dark and have stripes to help them hide when they are little. Because of damage to their habitat they are endangered. Some groups are trying to protect them.

The Golden Jackal

Golden Jackals live in parts of Africa and are quite common. Because there are so many of them, they often meet people and can be found near houses and farms. We need to learn how to live safely alongside this animal.

The African Elephant

The African Elephant is the world's largest land animal and can weigh as much as three family cars! Over many years, they have often been hunted by poachers and by farmers trying to protect their land. Now people are learning about how to live alongside this giant.

The Sumatran Orangutan

The Sumatran Orangutan lives in the trees of tropical rainforests. The trees they live in are being cut down for wood and the land is used to grow other things which means they are very endangered. There are not many of these animals left now.

Social Justice 9

Justice and injustice

Objective

SJE3.1A – Know about some of the causes and effects of injustice locally.

We will learn:

- what is meant by justice and injustice
- about injustice in our local area.

Key vocabulary

injustice, justice

i Social justice means being treated fairly and having access to what you need to live and thrive. This includes having enough food, water and money, a clean environment and a peaceful society.

There are impacts on people when they do not have these things.

Justice and injustice: Session 1

1 Draw lines to match the words with the descriptions.

| justice | treating someone unfairly |

| injustice | treating someone fairly |

2 Look at the words below. Use each word to complete the sentences.

fairly · food · live · money · peaceful

Social **justice** means treating everyone _____.

It means all people having what they need to _____ and thrive.

It includes having enough _____, water and _____.

Everyone should have a clean environment and a _____ society.

3 Tick the examples of social injustice.

☐ Homelessness
☐ Not being allowed to have a pet
☐ Not getting a new bike
☐ Families not having enough money for food

Justice and injustice: Session 1

4 Social injustice may occur in any local area. Here are two pictures showing some examples of this. Write a sentence in each box about the social injustice happening in each picture.

local social injustice

_____
_____
_____
_____

_____
_____
_____
_____

5 Choose one of the examples above. How does this local injustice make you feel?

_____
_____
_____

6 a) Describe at least two things children could do in this playground.

_____

_____

_____

b) Mateo uses a wheelchair. He wants to play too. What can he do?

_____

_____

_____

c) Will parts of the playground be tricky for Mateo? Is this fair? Why not?

_____

_____

_____

Justice and injustice: Session 1   13

7 Mateo cannot play on many things in the playground. Tick the boxes that show how he might feel.

☐ excited	☐ OK	☐ upset
☐ lucky		☐ lonely
☐ relieved		☐ frustrated

8 How could a playground be made suitable for everyone? Write an example in each box.

[_____]   [_____]

A playground suitable for everyone

[_____]   [_____]

What new things have you learned?
What had you not thought about before?

Social Justice

Wealth and poverty in society

Objective

SJE3.IB – Recognise the difference between wants and needs.

We will learn:
- to tell the difference between a want and a need
- to consider why certain things are a **necessity**.

Key vocabulary

entitled, necessity, need, want

ⓘ According to the United Nations Convention on the Rights of the Child (UNCRC) everyone is **entitled** to the things they need. We should be able to see the difference between the things we really need and the things we would like to have.

Wealth and poverty in society: Session 2   15

Here are some definitions of a **want** and a **need**.

A want is something you would like to have.

A need is something you cannot live without.

1 Write a short poem to help you remember the difference.

I want _____

I need _____

I want _____

I need _____

2 Complete each sentence with the correct word.

| want | need | need | want |

"I am very thirsty. Please may I have a drink?

I really _____ one," asked Milly.

"For my birthday, I _____ a new phone, please!" said Amir.

Aisha and Mel _____ to go to the shop to buy new toys.

I missed breakfast today, so I _____ to make sure I eat at lunchtime.

Wealth and poverty in society: Session 2

3 Put each of these in the correct box. Are they a need or a want? One has been done for you.

clean water	clean air	shelter	food
education	health care	toys	ball
mobile phone	computer	book	TV

Want	**Need**
	clean water

4 What are the differences between wants and needs?

_____
_____
_____
_____

Wealth and poverty in society: Session 2   17

5 Do you agree with Mo's statement?

We all need the same things to survive.

Write at least three things that all of us need so we can survive.

1 _____

2 _____

3 _____

What new things have you learned?
What had you not thought about before?

Equality of opportunity

Objective

SJE3.IC – Understand some of the barriers to equality of opportunity now and in the past.

We will learn:

- to recognise the barriers that prevent people being treated fairly and having equality of opportunity
- to understand that we have a personal responsibility to act fairly
- to show we can address unfairness.

Key vocabulary

disability, equality, fairly, opportunity, unfairness

i It is important that we recognise the barriers that prevent people being treated fairly and having **equality** of **opportunity** in society. We also need to be able to understand that we have a personal responsibility to act fairly and to be able to tackle **unfairness**.

Equality of opportunity: Session 3   19

1 Put a tick next to the barriers to people being treated **fairly**.

☐ A playground with no ramps for wheelchair users

☐ Someone having a guide dog that helps them get to work

☐ Not having access to an apartment with a lift

☐ Being banned from doing a job because of your **disability**

☐ Laws saying all people should be treated fairly

☐ Not being paid enough for your work

☐ Not being listened to when you need help with something

2 What can happen when someone is treated unfairly? Write a response, feeling or reaction in each box. One has been done for you.

☐

Someone might walk away.

☐

What happens when someone is treated unfairly?

☐

☐

Equality of opportunity: Session 3

3 Read the story and complete the sentences with 'fair' or 'unfair'.

Yusuf is nine years old. Today is his first day at a new school. He has hearing loss and wears a hearing aid.

a) The teacher keeps saying Yusuf's name incorrectly.

It is _____

because _____

_____.

b) Ahmet is asked to help him. He takes care of him and shows him around.

It is _____

because _____

_____.

c) Ahmet notices the hearing aid. He asks Yusuf if he needs any special help.

It is _____

because _____

_____.

d) At lunchtime, two boys begin teasing Yusuf.

It is _____

because _____

_____.

e) Ahmet tells them to go away and stop being nasty.

It is _____

because _____

_____.

f) Ahmet tells a teacher. The teacher says Yusuf and Ahmet should play somewhere else.

It is _____

because _____

_____.

Equality of opportunity: Session 3   21

4 a) Someone feels left out in the playground. What could you say to the person excluding them?

_____

_____

_____

b) What could you say to the person being excluded? Tick the possible answers.

- [ ] Everyone can join in with our games!
- [ ] I'm friends with everyone!
- [ ] Go away.
- [ ] If you have no one to play with, come and play with me!
- [ ] I don't like you.
- [ ] Come and join us!
- [ ] I would like to be your friend!
- [ ] Hey, let's play!

Equality of opportunity: Session 3

c) Draw a picture of your friends in the playground. What could they be saying to make everyone feel welcome in the playground? Try to include some speech bubbles!

What new things have you learned?

What had you not thought about before?

Challenging injustice

Social Justice — 23

Objective

SJE3.ID – Begin to recognise stereotypes, generalisations and assumptions and to understand that they can be harmful and inaccurate.

We will learn:

- the meaning of the words 'stereotype' and '**discrimination**'
- how to recognise stereotypes, **generalisations** and **assumptions**
- to recognise that they can be harmful.

Key vocabulary

assumptions, discrimination, generalisations, stereotype

i Sometimes, people can have fixed ideas about another group of people and they think that group of people are all the same. For example, someone might think that all girls like pink. This is a stereotype. We need to recognise when we see a stereotype, know that they can be harmful and have some ideas about how to tackle them.

1 Put the words in the correct place to explain what a **stereotype** is.

girls   same   stick

A stereotype is when you think that people who look similar are the _____.

A person who uses a stereotype may think that all _____ love the colour pink.

A person who uses a stereotype may think that all old people use a walking _____.

2 a) Tick the words you think best describe stereotyping.

☐ funny   ☐ unfair
☐ hurtful   ☐ wrong

b) Explain why you think this.

_____

_____

_____

3 a) Who can do these jobs? Circle **Yes**, **No** or **Don't know** in the table.

Job	Can any gender do this job?		
dancer	Yes	No	Don't know
firefighter	Yes	No	Don't know
doctor	Yes	No	Don't know
farmer	Yes	No	Don't know
teacher	Yes	No	Don't know
police officer	Yes	No	Don't know

b) Which of these jobs would you like to do?

_____

_____

c) How would you feel if someone suggested you were not suitable for one of the jobs because of your gender?

_____

_____

d) Draw a picture of you doing one of the jobs.

What new things have you learned?

What had you not thought about before?

Conflicts in the community

Peace and Conflict — 27

Objective

PC3.4A – Understand that our behaviour has consequences.

We will learn:

- how our behaviour has consequences
- to recognise how our behaviour can **affect** ourselves and others positively and negatively.

Key vocabulary

affect, consequence, effect

i How we behave has consequences. It is important to understand that some of these consequences are good and some are not so good. We need to understand the impact of our behaviour and the **effect** it may have on others.

Conflicts in the community: Session 1

1 Read the statements below and write True or False.

Statement	True or False?
Behaviour is the actions you do.	
Behaviour is only about doing bad things.	
Behaviour can be good or bad.	
Bad behaviour is when someone can be hurt by the things you do.	
Good behaviour can make you and others happy.	

Conflicts in the community: Session 1   29

2 Draw a happy or a sad face next to each situation below to show if you think the behaviour is good or bad.

Good behaviour	Bad behaviour

Behaviour	Good or bad?
Pushing someone over for not playing with you	
Not tidying up the things you have played with at home	
Helping a friend when they have fallen over	
Listening to an adult when they are talking	
Carrying someone's shopping bag when their hands are full	
Not feeding your pet	
Stealing from a shop	
Being rude to a teacher	

Conflicts in the community: Session 1

3 Read the middle column to find out about Neha's bad day! Write what has gone wrong in the left column. Write how you could help her have a better day in the right column.

What has gone wrong?	Neha's bad day	How could you help?
	Neha has argued with her mum. She gets to school late. She feels angry and upset and forgets her morning snack.	
	She finds out there's a test she did not know about. Her favourite lesson has been cancelled too.	
	She has to walk home on her own.	

4 a) Sometimes our actions can have bad **consequences** that we did not know would happen. We might feel sad and guilty because we did not mean to upset anyone.

Look at the short story below.

| Dad and Onur were in the garden. They decided that the tree was getting too big and it was blocking the sun. | Dad cut the tree down. | Mum came home and was sad that the tree was gone. She loved the tree and enjoyed sitting in the shade on hot days. |

b) What was the action? What was the consequence of the action?

_____

_____

_____

c) What could Dad and Onur have done to avoid the negative consequence?

_____

_____

_____

What new things have you learned?

What had you not thought about before?

Peace and Conflict

Resolving conflicts peacefully

Objective

PC3.4B – Know that resolving conflict requires a range of skills including compromise, seeing another point of view and using appropriate language.

We will learn:

- how to resolve conflicts peacefully
- to understand the need for seeing different points of view, compromising and using appropriate language in resolving conflicts.

Key vocabulary

compromising, conflict, peace, resolve, synonym

i Resolving conflicts needs many different skills including **compromising**, seeing other points of view and using language that does not upset anyone. It is helpful if we all learn how to do this.

Resolving conflicts peacefully: Session 2   33

1 Put the words in the correct place to define '**conflict**'.

| hurtful | **resolve** | bad | argument |

A conflict is a disagreement between people. It may cause an _____. Conflicts can make you feel very _____. People can say _____ things to each other during a conflict. You will feel much better when someone helps you to _____ your disagreement.

2 **Synonyms** are words that have a similar meaning to another word. 'Terrific' and 'great' both mean something is really good. Look at the words. Which words mean '**peace**' and which words mean '**conflict**'?

Write the words in the correct columns.

| argue | calm | restful | distress |

| tranquil | joy | disagree | fight |

Peace	Conflict

3 a) Look at the pictures below. Circle the one that you think shows conflict.

b) Look at the pictures below. Circle the one that shows a way to resolve conflict peacefully.

4 Elwina and Ryan are best friends, but have had a disagreement over how to play a game. How could they resolve this conflict? List your ideas below.

_____
_____
_____
_____

5 a) What skills do you have that you think could help to resolve a conflict?

_____
_____
_____

b) How could you improve your conflict resolution skills? For example, could you be more patient or give clearer instructions?

_____
_____
_____
_____

Resolving conflicts peacefully: Session 2

6 a) In order to resolve conflict, we need certain skills and we need to behave in a certain way. Tick the skills and behaviours you think are needed to resolve conflict.

- ☐ clear communication
- ☐ being dishonest
- ☐ trusting others
- ☐ being calm
- ☐ being angry
- ☐ showing aggression
- ☐ showing forgiveness
- ☐ being honest
- ☐ ignoring others
- ☐ being selfish
- ☐ listening carefully
- ☐ shouting

b) Look at the things you have ticked. Which three do you think are the most important? Write them below.

_____

_____

_____

_____

What new things have you learned?

What had you not thought about before?

Conflicts around the world

Objective

PC3.4C – Know about the role of United Nations (UN) Goodwill Ambassadors and Messengers of Peace.

We will learn:

- about the role of the United Nations Goodwill Ambassadors and Messengers of Peace.

Key vocabulary

global issue, United Nations Goodwill Ambassador, United Nations Messenger of Peace

i Conflicts can happen between you and family members, friends or peers. Did you know that there are bigger conflicts that happen around the world? Conflicts can be between a number of countries or about a **global issue** such as climate change. There are people who support organisations that help to keep the peace around the world. Let's find out more about them.

Conflicts around the world: Session 3

1 **UN Goodwill Ambassadors** and **Messengers of Peace** support organisations that keep peace around the world, give help to people in need and promote sustainable development. Do you know who some of these people are? Here is some information about two UN Goodwill Ambassadors and Messengers of Peace. Can you fill in the missing words for each person?

| music | leaders | Citizenship | China | three |

Lang Lang is a pianist who began playing the piano at the age of _____. He was born in _____. He has performed for many world _____. Lang Lang is interested in children's education and in particular in Global _____. He believes that _____ plays a very important part in children's lives and brings people together.

Conflicts around the world: Session 3

| countries | Tanzania | life |
| expert | chimpanzees | animals |

Jane Goodall has studied chimpanzees for most of her _____. She has spent 45 years in _____. She made some new discoveries about the behaviour of _____. She supports projects in one hundred _____. The projects help people, _____ and the environment. Jane Goodall is the world's greatest _____ on chimpanzees.

2 What would you do if you were a UN Goodwill Ambassador or Messenger of Peace? How would you behave? What would you focus on?

_____
_____
_____
_____

3 Here are two people who have been Goodwill Ambassadors or Messengers of Peace. Read about them and answer the questions.

a) Leonardo DiCaprio is an American actor. In 2004, he got the Clinton Global Citizen Award for his work. He believes that climate change can be reduced if all countries work together.

(i) What award did he get in 2004?

_____

(ii) What does he believe?

_____

b) Midori Goto wants all young people to do well and reach their goals. She has played the violin since she was three years old. She believes in the power of music to change people's lives.

(i) What does Midori want?

_____

(ii) What does she believe?

_____

What new things have you learned?
What had you not thought about before?

Sustainable Development 41

Planet Earth

Objective

SD3.7A – Know that there is an enormous variety of types of life and habitats on land and that they need to be protected.

We will learn:

- to appreciate the huge variety of life on planet Earth
- to understand that habitats must be protected.

Key vocabulary

habitat

ⓘ We are so lucky to share our world with beautiful and intelligent animals, creatures and plants of all sorts. Some of these are endangered and need protecting. Will you help protect them?

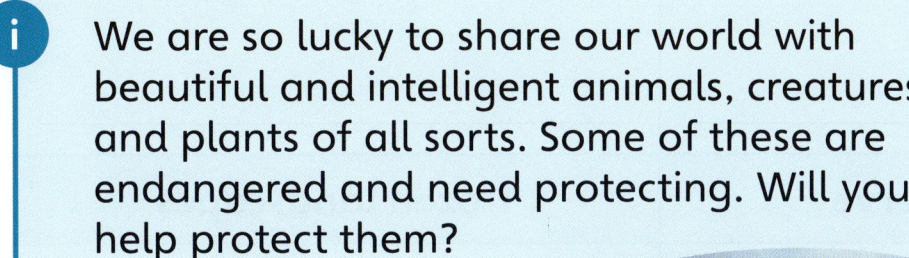

Planet Earth: Session 1

1 Here are six **habitats**. Which creatures or plants would you find in them? Draw and label a creature and plant in its habitat.

woodland	desert
pond	**garden**
wildlife reserve	**frozen landscapes**

Planet Earth: Session 1   43

2 Unscramble the words and then write where the animals live. You may need to do some research to help you find out.

G E R I T _____

Lives in: _____

L L A G R O I _____

Lives in: _____

P N D A A _____

Lives in: _____

O E A L P R D _____

Lives in: _____

3 There are many ways we can damage planet Earth. Look at the images and write why these activities are bad for the planet.

_____

_____

_____

_____

_____

_____

4 Can you think of any other human activities that are bad for the planet?

_____

_____

_____

5 Look at the logo and information for the UN Goal 15 'Life on Land'.

Look after forests, stop land being turned into deserts and wastelands, and look after all kinds of plants and animals.

Can you make a poster to advertise this goal? Write a sentence explaining why it is important.

_____

_____

What new things have you learned?
What had you not thought about before?

Connecting with nature (Greater Depth)

Objective

SD3.7B – Take pleasure in being outdoors.

We will learn:

- to appreciate the pleasures of being outdoors
- to appreciate what the outdoors has to offer.

Key vocabulary

mental well-being, outdoors

ⓘ When did you last spend time outdoors? What did you do? What did you see, hear and enjoy? Time outside can benefit our health and **mental well-being**. What's your favourite outdoor activity?

Connecting with nature: Session 2   47

1 Here is a space **outdoors**. What things could you do here? Draw an example in each box.

2 How often do you spend time outdoors? Tick one of the options below.

☐ Not often

☐ Only when I am going somewhere, for example to school

☐ Sometimes

☐ I always spend time outdoors!

3 Here are three different places outdoors. Complete the sentences below.

| The beach | Rainforest | Snowy mountains |

If I was at the beach I could

_____

_____.

If I was in the rainforest I could

_____

_____.

If I was on a snowy mountain I could

_____

_____.

The place I would most like to be out of all of these is

_____

_____.

This is because

_____

_____.

4 Go outside. Look around you and draw what you can see in the box.

5 Have you included all the creatures you have seen? Even the very smallest ones? What about the plants?

Maybe you can hear or see animals or birds and notice some footprints! Label your observations in your picture.

6 An acrostic poem is one where the first letter of each line spells out a word.

Create an acrostic poem for the word 'outdoors' in the box below.

You could start your poem with your own idea or use one from below:

- *Oh, what a lovely day it is!*
- *Orange, yellow and brown leaves fallen across the ground.*

O

U

T

D

O

O

R

S

What new things have you learned?
What had you not thought about before?

Sustainable Development   51

Biodiversity and habitat loss

Objective

SD3.7C – Understand how plants and animals support each other in the food chain.

We will learn:

- how the food chain works
- what food some creatures and plants need.

Key vocabulary

carnivore, consumer, food chain, herbivore, omnivore, prey

ⓘ The food chain shows how plants and animals get their energy. It starts with a green plant which is eaten by other living things. These living things are eaten by different living things. Where do you come in the food chain? Let's find out more.

A producer is a green plant that makes its own food from the sun.

A primary **consumer** is a creature that feeds on plants.

A secondary consumer is a creature that feeds on the primary consumers.

1 Draw a line to match the descriptions with the pictures.

producer

primary consumer

secondary consumer

2 A **food chain** looks like this:

Explain this food chain in your own words.

_____
_____
_____

A **herbivore** is an animal that feeds on plants.

A **carnivore** is an animal that feeds on other animals.

An **omnivore** is an animal that eats both plants and animals.

3 Draw a line to match the animal types in the food chain to their definitions.

carnivore	A bear eats both plants and meat.
herbivore	A tiger only eats other animals.
omnivore	An elephant eats plants.

4 Write the names of these living things into the correct place on the diagram to complete the food chain.

frog   bird of **prey**   grasshopper   leaves

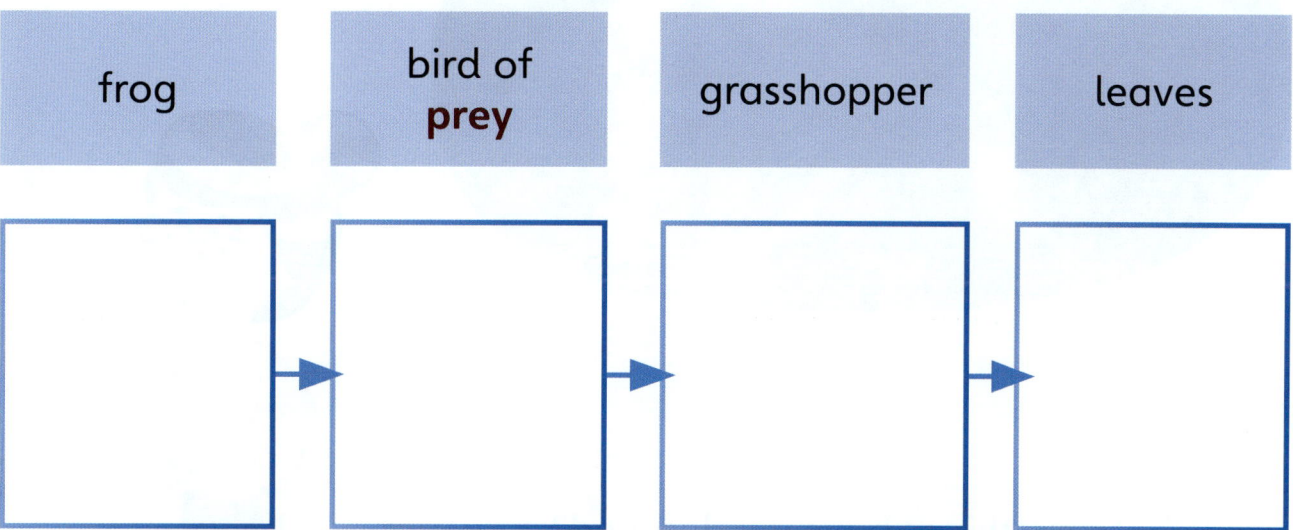

5 a) Some baby birds are fed caterpillars by their parents. Many caterpillars eat the leaves of trees. A large tree has been cut down to make way for a new road. What does this mean for the baby birds in this area? How will the food chain be affected?

_____

_____

_____

b) What arguments about protecting the food chain could you use to protect trees in your area?

_____

_____

What new things have you learned?

What had you not thought about before?

Sustainable Development 55

Climate change (Greater Depth)

Objective

SD3.7D – Understand that addressing climate change requires everyone working together to find a solution.

We will learn:

- what climate change is
- to think of solutions to deal with climate change
- how these issues can be dealt with **collaboratively**.

Key vocabulary

climate, collaboratively, fossil fuels, solution

ⓘ Our world's climate is changing at a faster rate than ever before because of human activity. We all have a duty to protect our world and we need to work together to achieve this. How will you help?

56 Climate change: Session 4

1 Here is an example of what damage is happening in our world due to **climate** change. Look at the picture below and describe what you can see.

_____

_____

_____

2 Which of the actions below contribute to climate change? Tick all of the actions you think are bad for the climate.

- ☐ Going to school by car
- ☐ Wasting food
- ☐ Eating meat
- ☐ Turning the air conditioning up high
- ☐ Leaving the television on standby
- ☐ Cutting down trees

Climate change: Session 4   **57**

3 Look at the list in Activity 2. What can you do to reduce climate change? Draw and label your ideas below. One problem and one **solution** have been done for you.

Travelling to school by car	Walking to school

        The problem   **The solution**

Climate change: Session 4

4 What is climate change? Complete the following sentences using the words in the boxes.

| flooding | gas | extinct | weather | oil |

| coal | fires | rising | melting |

Climate change means that the _____ is becoming more unpredictable.

Temperatures in many places are _____.

This causes _____ of ice caps in some places and forest _____ in other places.

It also causes terrible storms and _____.

Climate change is also causing a lot of plants and creatures to become _____.

What is causing climate change?

Human behaviour, such as burning **fossil fuels** like _____, _____ and _____ causes harmful gases to be released into the atmosphere.

Climate change: Session 4   59

5 Some people don't believe that climate change is happening. They don't think they will be affected.

Here is Karma. He says this:

I am not worried about climate change! I have enough to eat and drink and I am not very interested in what is happening in different places. Sometimes it may be too hot and sometimes it may be too cold, but I don't mind.

Karma does not understand climate change.
Can you explain it to him?

_____
_____
_____
_____
_____

What new things have you learned?
What had you not thought about before?

Energy, pollution, waste and recycling

> **Objective**
>
> **SD3.7E** – Know about the benefits of recycling, reusing, repairing, remodelling, refusing.

We will learn:

- how to be more sustainable by reducing, recycling, reusing, repairing, remodelling and refusing
- about the benefits of reducing, recycling, reusing, repairing, remodelling and refusing.

Key vocabulary

recycle, reduce, refuse, remodel, repair, reuse

ⓘ Have you ever turned an empty box into a play den or perhaps a garage for your toy cars? If you have, then you have reused it. What do you do with other unwanted items?

Energy, pollution, waste and recycling: Session 5

1 Here are some pictures showing things which have been reused, remodelled, recycled, repaired, reduced and refused. Write the correct word for each picture.

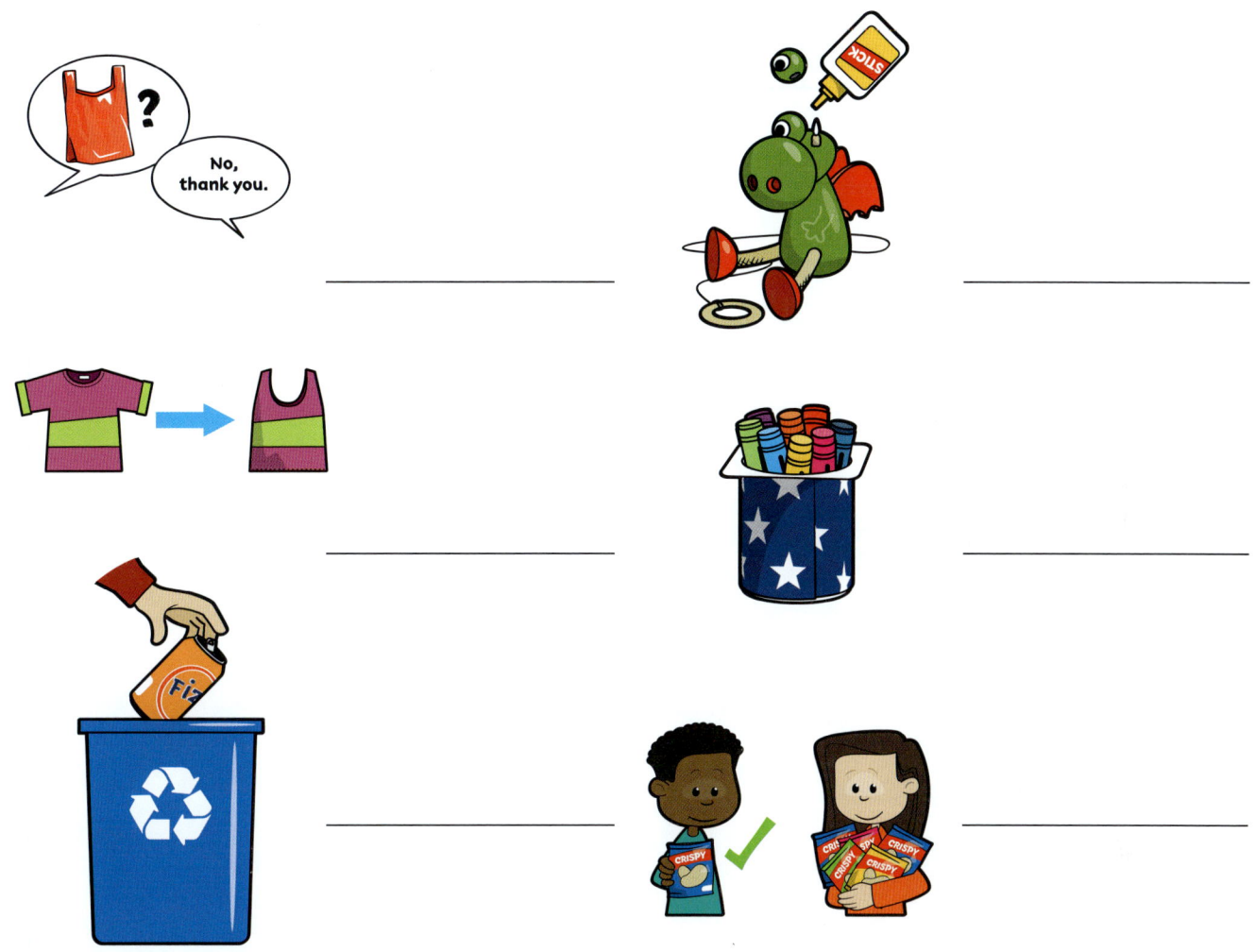

2 Unscramble the letters below to spell out six ways we can be more sustainable.

R C L E E Y C _____

R F S E E U _____

R E E C U D _____

R P R E I A _____

M D L E O R E _____

S E E U R _____

3 Look at the six actions in Activity 2. Choose one of the six actions and create a poster that persuades people to either **reuse**, **recycle**, **reduce**, **repair**, **refuse** or **remodel**.

4 Describe what you can see in the picture.

_____

_____

_____

5 Design something new using materials that may be thrown away. Draw your design below.

6 Temwe and her family have just moved house. There are a lot of empty cardboard boxes. Temwe has asked to keep one of the boxes. List at least four things she could do with it.

_____

_____

_____

_____

What new things have you learned?

What had you not thought about before?

Sustainable Development 65

The future of our planet

Objective

SD3.7F – Know what sustainability means.

We will learn:
- what sustainability means
- the importance of being sustainable.

Key vocabulary

compromising, generations, sustainability

i Our world is precious and needs to be looked after with great care. We need to act responsibly and urgently in order to protect it and all of its natural resources, for us and for future generations. We all need to play our part.

1 Read the definition of **sustainability**. Write each word into the text to complete the sentences.

present   needs   future

Sustainability is about meeting the _____ of people in the _____ without **compromising** the ability of _____ **generations** to meet their needs.

2 Which pictures show ways of being sustainable? How do you know? Write what you think below.

_____
_____
_____
_____

3 Who and what would benefit from you behaving more sustainably?

Use the pictures to help you write a paragraph sharing your ideas.

_____

_____

_____

_____

What new things have you learned?

What had you not thought about before?

Who am I?

Identity and Diversity

> **Objective**
>
> **ID3.2A** – Have a sense of identity and self-esteem.

We will learn:

- what is meant by self-esteem
- how to explore our own identity and be proud of it
- how believing in ourselves can have a positive effect on our mental well-being.

Key vocabulary

self-esteem, unique, value

i Everyone is **unique** and has **value**. Self-esteem means valuing yourself and knowing that you are great. Being kind to yourself can help to promote self-esteem. Think about an inspirational quote that you can tell yourself to help boost your self-esteem; for example: *you can do it, you are strong, your mistakes are making you stronger*. Practise saying this quote to yourself every day.

Who am I? Session 1   69

1 Read the statements. Write your name and complete the sentences with a word from below.

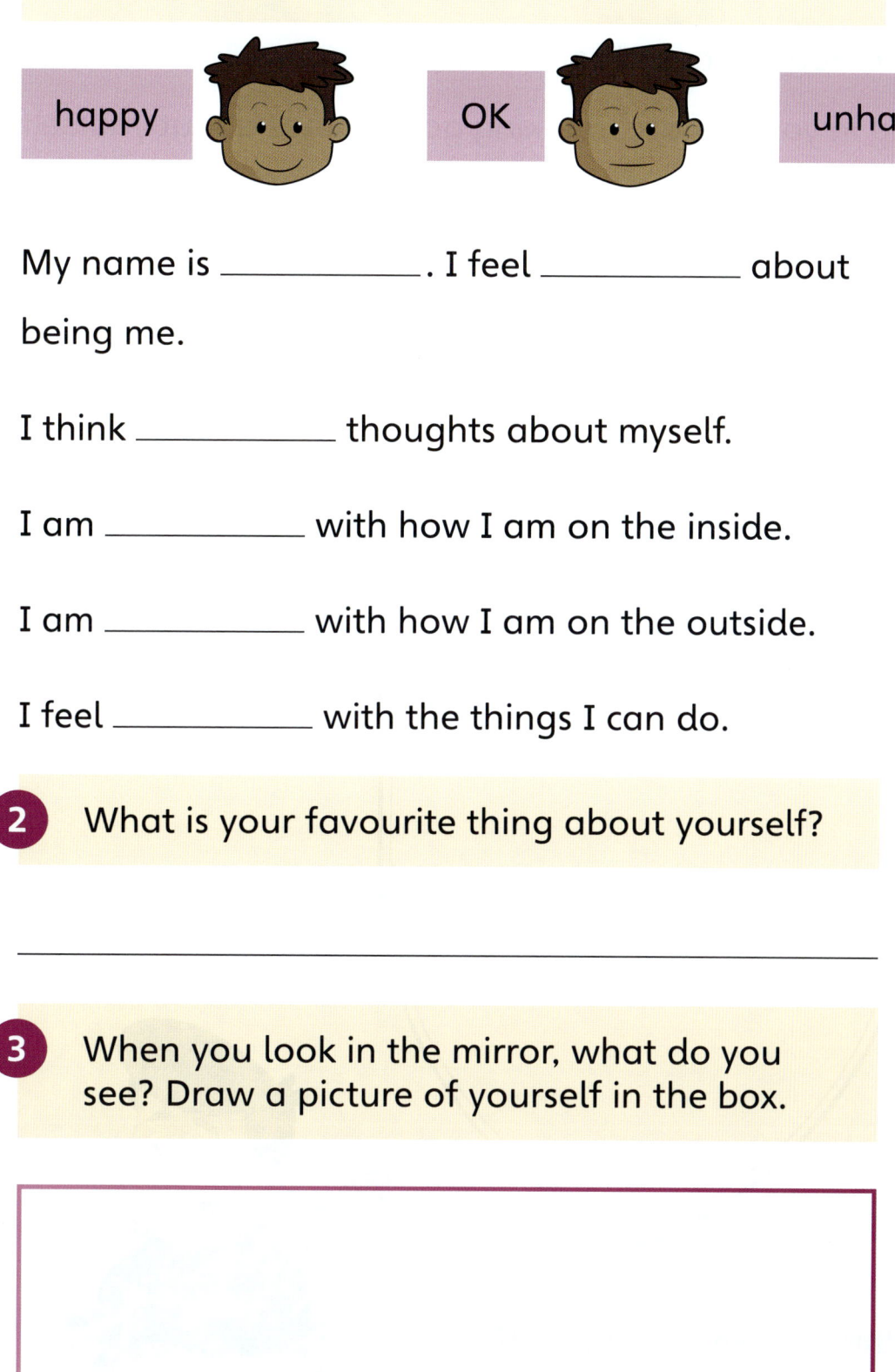

happy   OK   unhappy

My name is _____. I feel _____ about being me.

I think _____ thoughts about myself.

I am _____ with how I am on the inside.

I am _____ with how I am on the outside.

I feel _____ with the things I can do.

2 What is your favourite thing about yourself?

_____

3 When you look in the mirror, what do you see? Draw a picture of yourself in the box.

Who am I? Session I

4 Read the list below. Tick the phrase that best describes **self-esteem**.

☐ Worrying about what others think of you

☐ Believing in yourself and thinking good things about yourself

☐ Wishing you were more like someone else

5 This shield protects you from being hurt. When our feelings are hurt, if we can remember what makes us great, it can protect us and help to make us feel better.

Write positive words and phrases into the shield that describe you.

What new things have you learned?
What had you not thought about before?

Humankind: all equal; all different

Identity and Diversity — 71

Objective

ID3.2B – Be able to make connections with others who seem different from them.

We will learn:

- that there are similarities between everyone
- how to make connections with others.

Key vocabulary

connections, differences, similarities, unique

ⓘ All human beings have similarities. Some of us have the same hair colour, speak the same language, like the same activities – and we all breathe the same air. It is fun to see how many **connections** you can make with someone else!

1 Let's look closely at finding **similarities** and **differences**. How many similarities can you find between these two pictures?

2 a) Mya and Tommy are best friends. Look carefully at both of them. What similarities can you spot? Write them in the middle of the Venn diagram. One has been done for you.

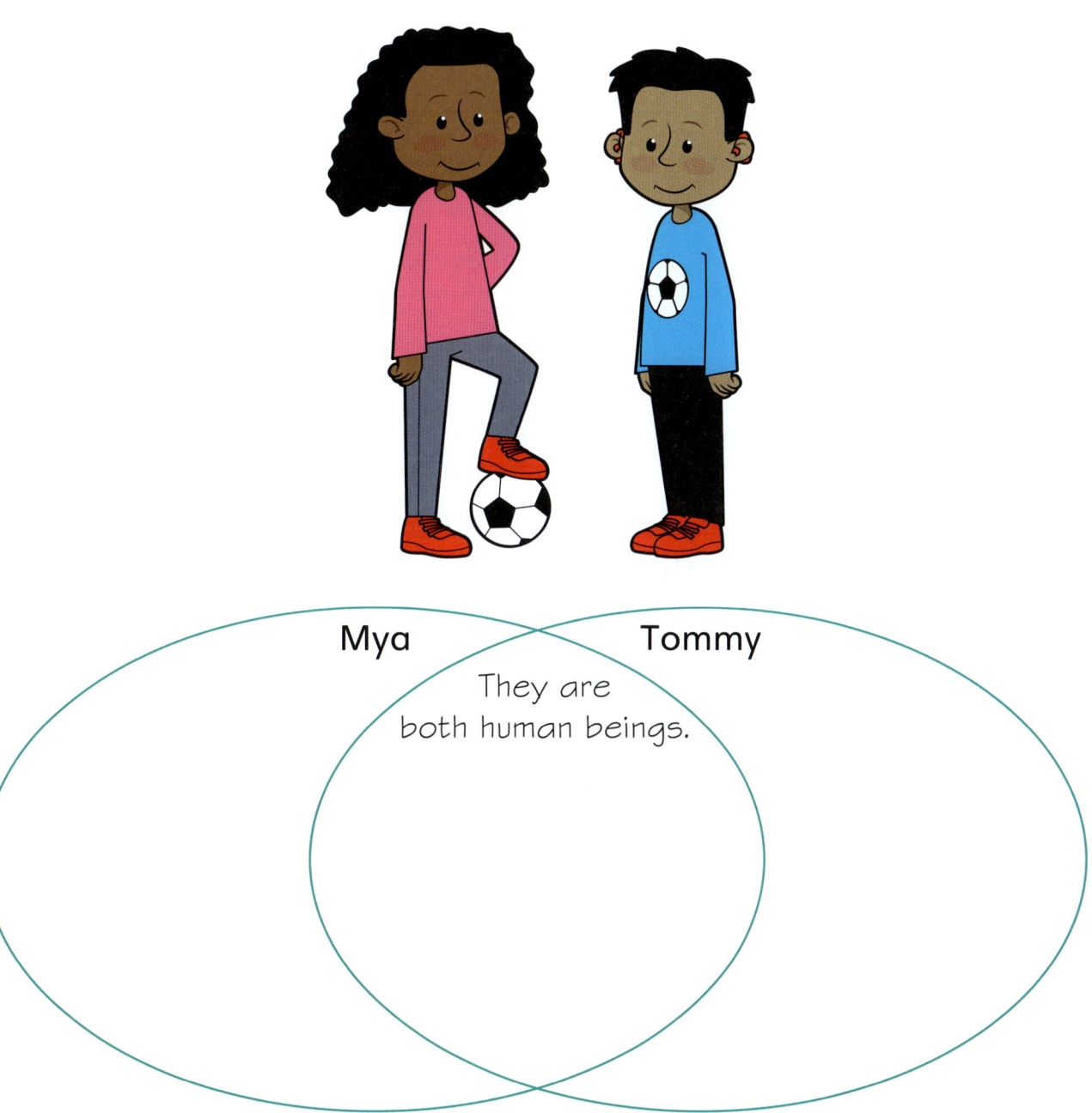

b) What differences can you see between Mya and Tommy? Write the things that only apply to Mya on her side of the Venn diagram and only to Tommy on his side.

3 **a)** Why is it good to have similarities?

_____

_____

_____

b) Why is it good to have differences?

_____

_____

_____

4 Think about one of your friends. What do you like about them? Do you think they like you for the same reasons? Write the similarities between you and your friend in the middle of the Venn diagram and the differences on the left and right. One similarity has been done for you.

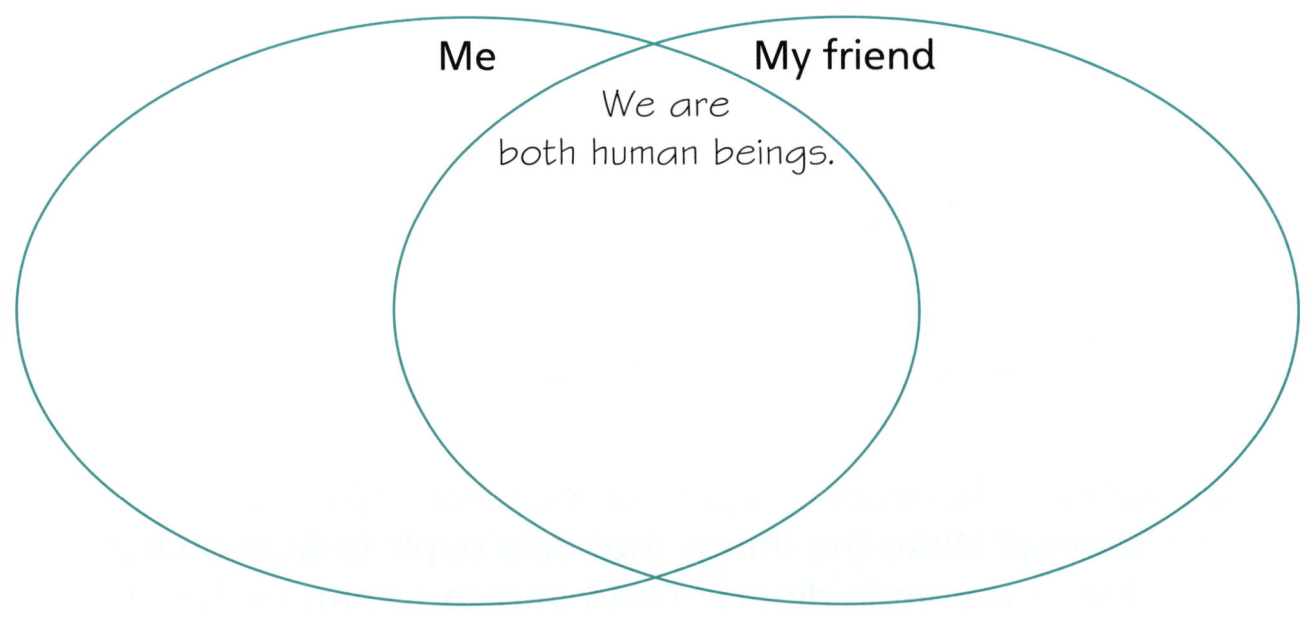

5 Write each word into the speech bubble to complete Mya's description of similarities and differences between us.

similarities   **unique**   all

connect   differences   love

There are _____ and _____ between us and _____ the people we meet. The similarities _____ us and the differences make us _____.
I _____ being unique!

6 A new girl has just started at your school. You would like to play with her, but she is very shy. She speaks many languages, but she is just beginning to learn English. What should you do? How could you become good friends?

What new things have you learned?
What had you not thought about before?

Challenging prejudice and discrimination

Objective

ID3.2C – Know how to support classmates who have experienced prejudice.

We will learn:

- how to define and recognise prejudice
- the negative effects of prejudice
- how to **support** our classmates who experience prejudice.

Key vocabulary

judgements, prejudice, support, unfairly

ⓘ Having negative ideas about someone or a group of people without knowing them is called prejudice. Prejudice is judging people **unfairly**. Making unkind and untrue assumptions about someone when you do not know them can also hurt their feelings.

Challenging prejudice and discrimination: Session 3 — 77

1 a) Look at the person below. What assumptions might people have about this person? Write an idea in each box.

| I think his favourite colour is _____. | I think he would like _____. |

| I think he is good at _____. | I think he is not good at _____. |

b) How do you know the things you have written are true?

_____
_____
_____

c) Why can't we answer questions about someone by just looking at them?

_____
_____
_____

2 What can you do if you see **prejudice** happening in your class?

How can you help someone who this has happened to?

Circle all the ways you can help.

Explain to the person showing prejudice that what they are saying is not true.

Tell an adult that someone is being unkind to your friend.

Show your friend that you care by trying to make them happy.

Tell your friend that it is just a joke and that prejudice is funny.

Tell your friend to deal with it themselves.

Decide not to get involved.

Make sure you stick up for your friend.

3 The things we read and see around us can make us think the wrong things about other people. Most of the time, people do not realise they are being prejudiced.

Can you create a recipe to help stop prejudice? Write the ingredients you think you need in your recipe to help stop prejudice.

_____

_____

_____

_____

_____

_____

_____

4 Think about what you have learned. Think about how you would feel if you could help someone challenge prejudice. To do this, you need to try to make sure you are not prejudiced in any way. How can you do this?

Write a sentence to say how you will listen better to stop prejudice.

_____

_____

Write a sentence to say how you will say sorry if you are prejudiced towards someone.

_____

_____

Write a sentence to say how you will get to know someone better and will not make **judgements** about them.

_____

_____

What new things have you learned?

What had you not thought about before?

Globalisation and Interdependence | 81

People and places around the world (Greater Depth)

Objective

GI3.3A – Know that there are similarities between every country in the world.

We will learn:

- to recognise that there are many similarities between countries
- to appreciate that all countries have a capital city, towns and rural areas.

Key vocabulary

currency, similarities

i) The world is made up of many different countries. One very interesting thing is that there are similarities between every single one of them. Can you find all the connections?

People and places around the world: Session 1

1 Complete each box about either the country you live in, or the country you were born in.

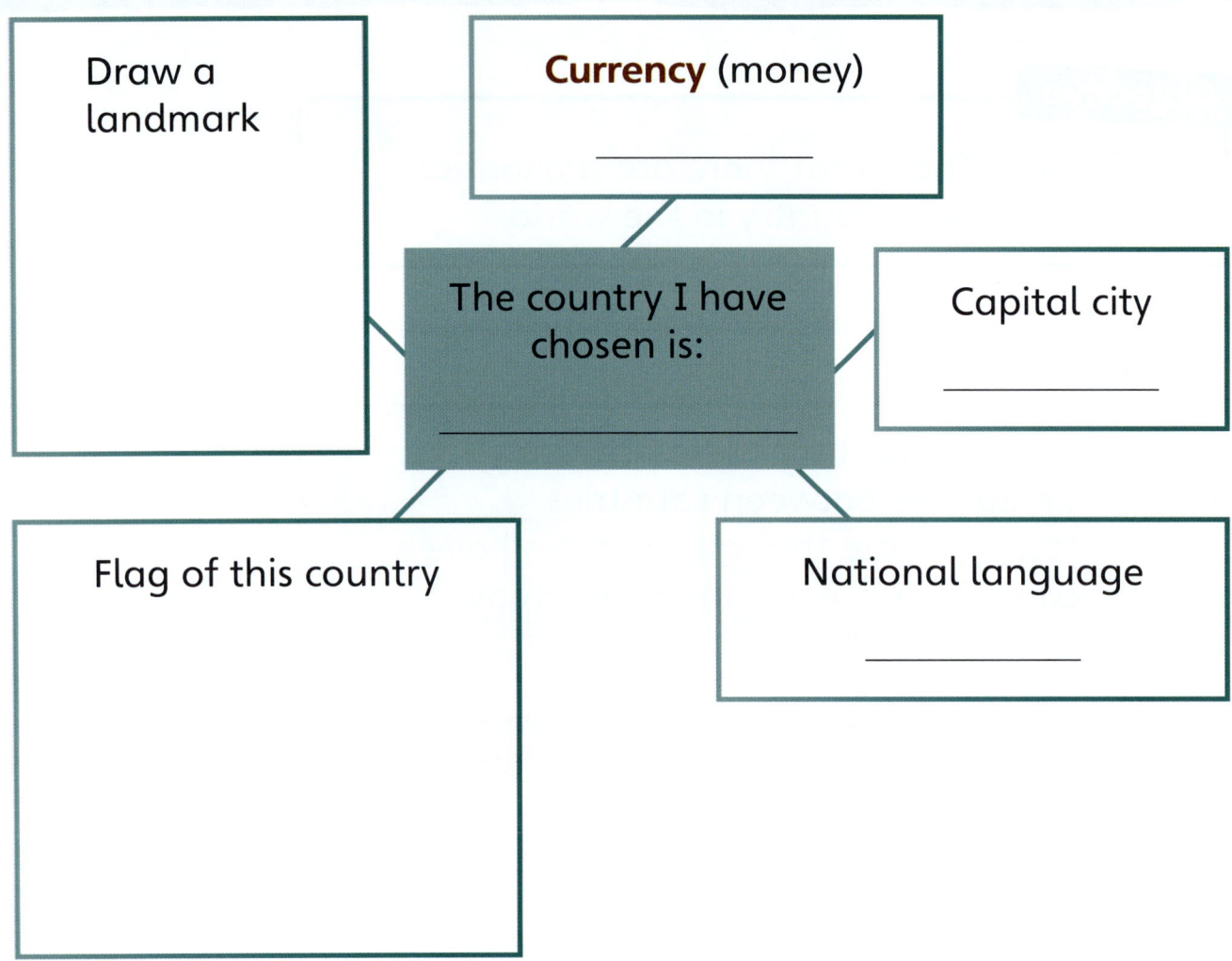

2 Countries have many **similarities**. Tick the things that you think **all** countries have.

☐ at least one national language
☐ jobs
☐ education
☐ people

☐ a capital city
☐ hospitals
☐ money (currency)
☐ animals

3 Look again at the things you ticked in Activity 2. All countries around the world have these things in common. Does this surprise you? Did you know this?

Which country would you love to visit? Why? Complete the sentences below.

I would like to visit _____.

I would like to see the _____
_____.

I have heard it has _____
_____.

I want to find out more about _____
_____.

4 a) Think of the names of three countries that have a lot of snow. Write them in the snow globe below. One has been done for you.

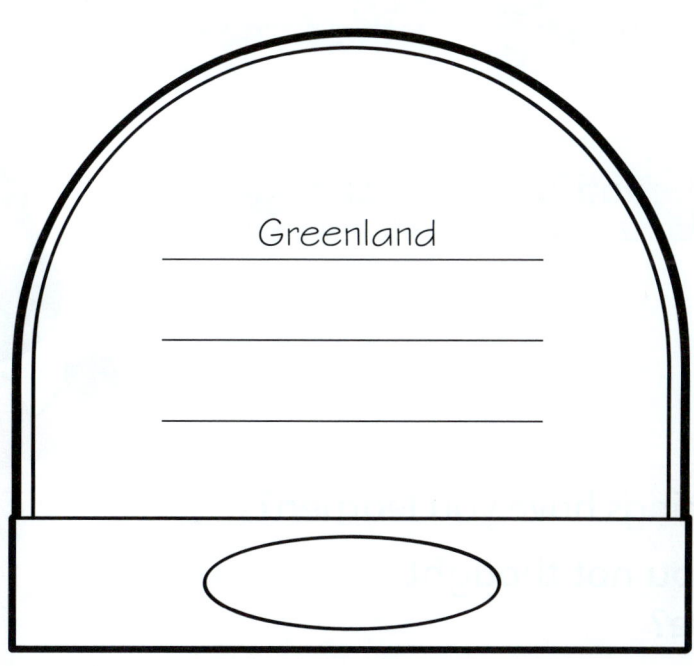

Greenland

b) Think of the names of three countries which have a lot of sun. Write them in the sun. One has been done for you.

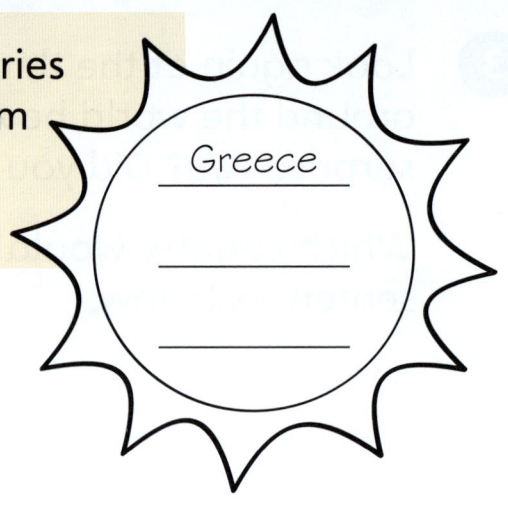

Greece

c) Think of the names of three countries which have a lot of rain. Write them in the raindrop. One has been done for you.

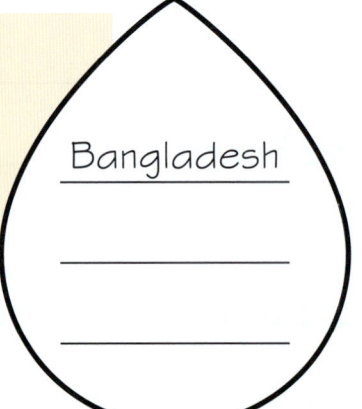

Bangladesh

5 Circle the words that describe all the countries of the world.

similar   unique   the same

diverse   beautiful   special

What new things have you learned?
What had you not thought about before?

Globalisation and Interdependence — 85

Global trade, ethics, production and consumption

Objective

GI3.3B – Begin to understand what it means to be a responsible consumer.

We will learn:

- to understand what it means to be a responsible consumer
- to consider if you really need everything you buy.

Key vocabulary

consumer, landfill, need, responsible, want

ⓘ People are consumers. This means that we buy things that other people make or grow. Being a responsible consumer means that we think about the people that make or grow the things we buy and how this affects the environment. Through only buying the things we need and swapping toys and games we no longer want with each other, we can be responsible consumers.

Global trade, ethics, production and consumption: Session 2

1 What does it mean to be **responsible**? Draw a line to match the sentences with the words.

Leaving the door open on a cold day

Wasting food

Helping an adult to tidy up

Leaving the tap running when you are cleaning your teeth

Turning the lights off when you are not in the room

Looking after your family members

Telling a lie

responsible

irresponsible

2 What does it mean to be a responsible **consumer**? Circle **Yes** or **No**.

Being responsible is about making good choices that help everyone.	Yes No
A responsible consumer puts all their rubbish in the bin that is going to **landfill**.	Yes No
A responsible consumer thinks about their actions and wants to make the world a better place.	Yes No
Being responsible is about only buying the things you really **need**.	Yes No
A responsible consumer has many pairs of trainers in different colours and styles.	Yes No
A responsible consumer swaps their toys and games with their friends.	Yes No

3 We all have a responsibility to look after each other and the world by saving resources and treating people and planet Earth with care. How could you be a more responsible consumer? Draw or write one thing you will do differently to become a more responsible consumer.

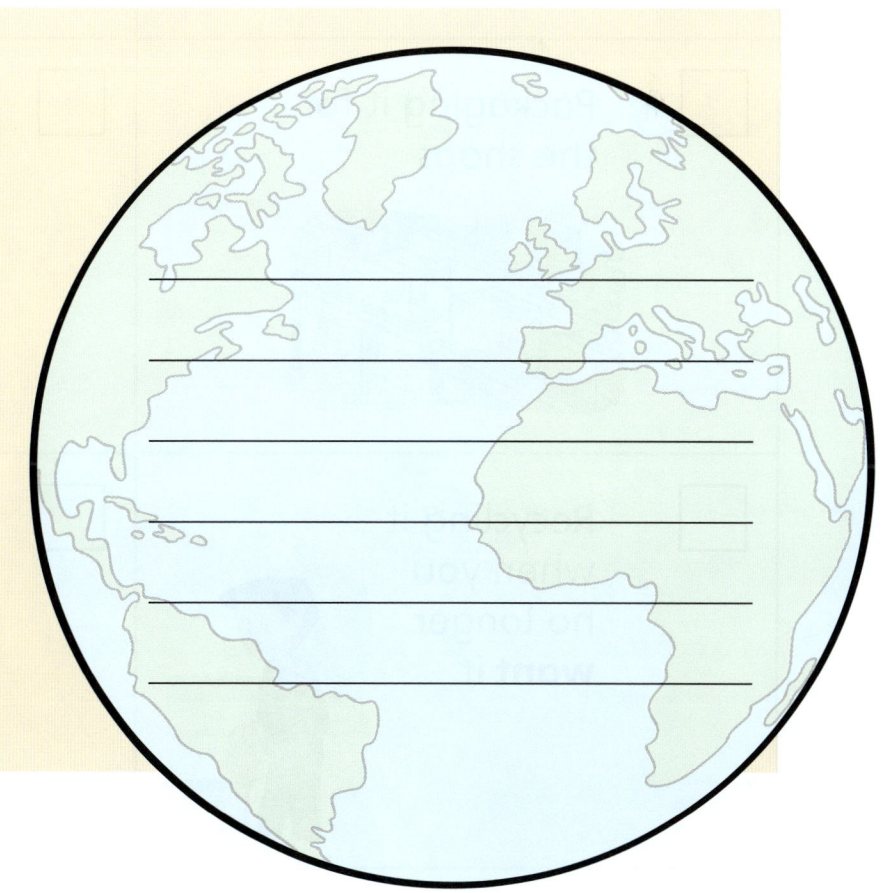

88 Global trade, ethics, production and consumption: Session 2

4 Look at the stages needed to make a cotton T-shirt. Number the stages in the correct order to create a lifecycle of a T-shirt.

☐ Harvesting the cotton	☐ Sending it to the shops
☐ Washing it at home	☐ Dyeing it
☐ Packaging it for the shops	☐ Using the cotton to make a T-shirt
☐ Recycling it when you no longer **want** it	☐ Buying it

5 Buying things we do not need uses up our planet's valuable resources.

Look at the lifecycle of a T-shirt again. Can you explain why it is bad to buy too many things that we don't really need?

_____

_____

_____

6 Look at each action below. Draw a line to match the sentences with the phrases.

Buying three of the same coat because you wanted one in each colour

Giving your toys to charity for someone to reuse

Throwing a meal away because you already ate when you were out

Freezing food so that it does not go to waste

responsible action

irresponsible action

What new things have you learned?
What had you not thought about before?

Global wealth and poverty

Globalisation and Interdependence

Objective

GI3.3C – Know that there is more to wealth than money.

We will learn:

- that being wealthy is not just about having lots of money
- to recognise the different ways in which you can be wealthy.

Key vocabulary

expensive, wealthy

i Having lots of money makes you wealthy. Having trusted, great friends makes you wealthy. Having love in your life makes you wealthy. Having enough to eat and drink before you go to sleep makes you wealthy. In which ways are you wealthy?

1 What does being **wealthy** mean to you?
Choose three things from the list below to draw.

I have people that love me.

I have people that look after me.

I have money to buy things.

I have food to eat.

I have a place to live.

I have enough to drink.

I have books to read and a school to go to.

I have friends.

I have fresh air to breathe.

2 Soo has a lot of lovely things happening in her life, but this has not made her happy. What is making her unhappy? What kind of 'wealth' seems to be missing from her life?

> My parents are wealthy. We have lots of money, **expensive** clothes and cars, and we go on many holidays to different countries. I often feel sad and lonely.

_____

_____

_____

_____

What new things have you learned?
What had you not thought about before?

Globalisation and Interdependence   93

Information, technology and communication

Objective

GI3.3D – Be able to tell fact from fiction and opinion.

We will learn:

- to define fact and fiction
- how to tell the difference between fact, fiction and opinion.

Key vocabulary

fact, opinion

i) It is important to be able to tell the difference between fact, fiction and opinion because we need to know what is true and what is made up. Fiction is something that is made up and non-fiction is something that is a fact. An opinion is someone's idea that may or may not be true.

When is your birthday? How can you prove that date is your birthday? Perhaps you have a passport or birth certificate to prove it. Something you can prove is a fact. Factual writing is called non-fiction. Things that are made up, like stories, are fiction. What is your favourite fictional film or book?

Information, technology and communication: Session 4

1 Write a list of some non-fiction and fiction books or films.

Non-fiction (true events)	Fiction (not true)
• _____	• _____
• _____	• _____
• _____	• _____
• _____	• _____
• _____	• _____

2 Look at the picture of the tiger. Can you list more **facts** about tigers? One has been done for you.

Facts about tigers
1 Tigers have tails.
2 _____
3 _____
4 _____

Your **opinion** is something that you think or believe, but it may be different from what others think or believe. These children are giving their opinions about their favourite food.

I love pizza! It is the best food ever!

No way! Watermelon is by far the best food in the world.

Both children are right, they just have different opinions.

3 List yours and another person's opinion in the table.

My opinion	_____'s opinion
The best fruit is _____.	The best fruit is _____.
The best drink is _____.	The best drink is _____.
The best colour is _____.	The best colour is _____.
The best animal is _____.	The best animal is _____.

4 Read each statement below and tick the correct box to show if it is fact, fiction or opinion.

	Fact	Fiction	Opinion
"I have the best mum in the world!" yelled Miran.			
Whales are mammals and they give birth to their young.			
There are seven continents in the world.			
The unicorn lives in the forest made of sweets.			
Joseph thinks that cats are the cutest animals.			

What new things have you learned?

What had you not thought about before?

Global health, food and well-being

Globalisation and Interdependence — 97

Objective

GI3.3E – Know where our food comes from, locally and globally.

We will learn:

- to recognise that we rely on food from both local and global **sources**
- how to appreciate that we live in an interdependent world.

Key vocabulary

climate, expertise, interconnected, local, produced, source, space

i Our world today is more **interconnected** than ever. We all rely on food produced in many other countries. This is called interdependence. What does your local area produce?

1. Look at this map of where fruit grows around the world.

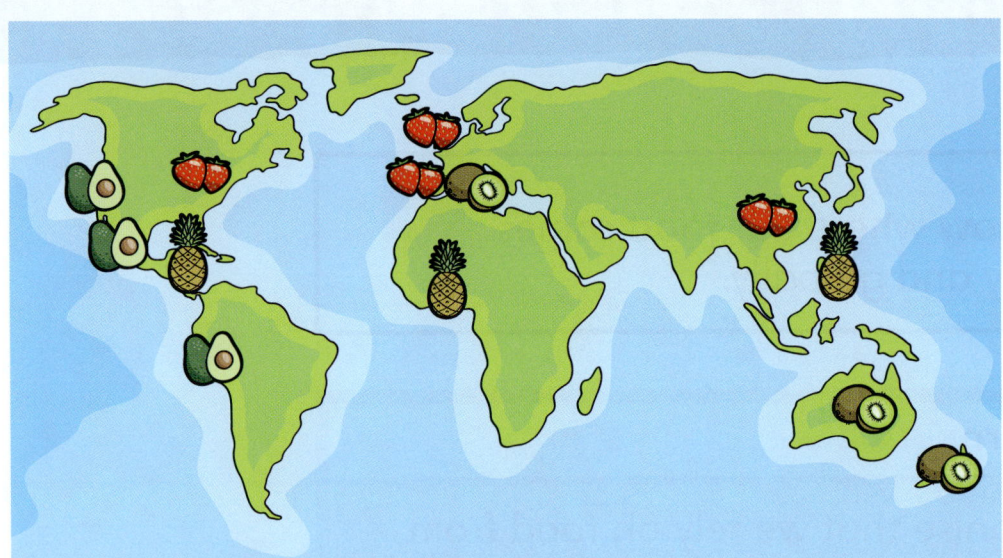

2. Look at the map again. Where do these fruits come from?

| Asia | Africa | North America |

| South America | Europe | Central America |

| Australia and New Zealand |

Fruit	Where from?
kiwi fruit	
avocado	
strawberry	
pineapple	

3 Do you know what food items are **produced** in your **local** area or country? Draw them here.

4 There are different reasons why an area or country produces certain items. Draw a line to match the reasons to the words.

| Some produce can only grow well in the right conditions. | space |

| Some countries have large areas of land to grow a lot of produce. | expertise |

| Some crops have been grown in a certain area or country for years. This makes the people there very knowledgeable. | climate |

5 What is good about being able to share produce and resources around the world?

_____

_____

6 Can you think of any difficulties with relying on another country's produce and resources?

_____

What new things have you learned?
What had you not thought about before?

Understanding rights

Objective

HR3.5A – Know some key articles from the UNCRC and how rights relate to life in school, at home and beyond.

We will learn:

- how all children have rights
- to recognise some key articles from the UNCRC and how they relate to our lives.

Key vocabulary

rights, United Nations Convention of the Rights of the Child (UNCRC)

i All children in the world have rights. These rights help us to keep safe and healthy. Children may need support in order to access these rights. The people who look after you must ensure that you have the things you need. Who looks after you?

1 What do you know about Children's **Rights**?

What would you like to know?

Write your ideas in the table below. Once you have completed this session, you can add in what you have learned.

What I know:	What I would like to know:	What I have learned:

2 a) Why is it important to have the right to play?

b) Why is it important to have the chance to talk about how you feel and be listened to?

___

___

c) Why is it important that no one harms you?

___

___

3 The **United Nations Convention on the Rights of the Child (UNCRC)** is a list of all the rights that the United Nations believe all children should have. These rights have been agreed by almost every country of the world. Look at some of the rights. How many of these do you have?

Survival	Development	Participation	Protection

You have a right to life, water, good food and to grow up healthy.	You have a right to education, play and relaxation.	You have a right to express how you feel and to be listened to.	You have a right to be treated with respect and not to be hurt by another person.

___

___

___

4 The UNCRC includes rights that apply to children when they are at home, at school and elsewhere. Adults and governments should make sure children have these rights in their country.

Tick the rights a child's carer or the government should make sure they have.

	Carer	Government
Every child has the right to an education. Primary education must be free and different forms of secondary education must be available to every child.	☐	☐
Every child has the right to be registered at birth, to have a name and nationality and, as far as possible, to know and be cared for by their parents.	☐	☐
Every child has the right to life. Governments must do all they can to ensure that children survive and develop to their full potential.	☐	☐

What new things have you learned?
What had you not thought about before?

Violation of rights

Human Rights — 105

Objective

HR3.5B – Be able to recognise, name and challenge bullying behaviour.

We will learn:

- how to recognise, name and challenge bullying behaviour
- the damage caused by bullying.

Key vocabulary

behaviour, bullying, response

i Bullying is **behaviour** that makes people feel miserable and isolated. People who behave in this way need to be challenged. We need to know how to recognise this behaviour in order to challenge it. The adults in school are there to protect you if you are being bullied.

Violation of rights: Session 2

1 Put the words in the correct place to complete the definition of **bullying**.

human rights	mentally	group
physically	person	cruel
continuously	online	damage

Bullying is when one _____ or a _____ of people _____ hurt someone _____ or _____. This can be done in person, indirectly or _____. Bullying is a _____ act that can cause _____. Bullying is denying one's _____ _____.

2 Read the examples below and tick which ones are examples of bullying.

- ☐ Accidentally tripping a friend over
- ☐ Always making fun of a person you do not like
- ☐ Repeatedly calling someone unkind names
- ☐ Giving horrible looks to a group of children
- ☐ Having an argument with your friend
- ☐ Sharing a book with a friend
- ☐ Hiding someone's lunch or book bag every day, even though the child gets upset
- ☐ Copying a friend's work when you do not know the answer

3 Here is Murat. This is what he thinks about bullies:

> I can always spot bullies! They always wear dark-coloured clothes, have angry facial expressions and will hurt anyone they walk past. I keep away from anyone who I see who looks like this.

Do you agree with Murat's statement? Can you always tell someone's character or intention by what they look like? Explain why in your answer and try to use examples.

_____
_____
_____
_____
_____
_____
_____
_____

Violation of rights: Session 2

4 Gita notices some older children laughing at Dechen and bullying her during playtime. The children are calling her nasty names and Dechen is crying. Gita is worried, but she does not know what to do. Are the older children bullying Dechen?

☐ Yes ☐ No

5 Can Gita help Dechen? Circle which of the following options you think Gita should do.

Be horrible to the older children, ask your friends to join in with you.

Speak to an adult about what is going on right away.

Just ignore it. The school bell is about to ring and it will be time to go in.

6 Draw or write what you would do next.

Violation of rights: Session 2   109

Bullying does not just affect the person or people it is done to. It affects everyone involved, such as family members and other friends. Bullying is very serious and we should never do it. But it is also important to remember that those who bully others are usually not happy themselves. They are often dealing with very sad and angry things and use bullying as a way to deal with them.

7 If Dechen's bullying was not dealt with by the teachers at school, things would be very difficult. She might go home and shout at her family. She might hide in her room.

Complete the table to show how the people listed could be affected by this bullying. One has been done for you.

Who is affected?	How are they affected?
The group of children who have been bullying Dechen	The children who bullied Dechen will not be feeling very good about their actions
Dechen's parents	
Dechen's brother or sister	
Dechen's friends	
Dechen herself	

What new things have you learned?
What had you not thought about before?

Refugees, asylum seekers and internally displaced people

Objective

HR3.5C – Have ability and desire to show interest in people from different backgrounds from their own.

We will learn:

- to show **interest** in people from different backgrounds from our own
- why someone becomes a refugee.

Key vocabulary

differences, interest, refugee, similarities

ⓘ It is always really interesting and exciting to meet people from different backgrounds to our own. Life may have been complicated for some, including those who have had to leave their country for their own safety. There is always a lot we can learn from other people's experiences.

Here are some groups of friends and families. You may be able to see some **similarities** and **differences** between them already, which is great! But there are things about each individual that you can learn more about by asking questions. For example, you won't know where they were born, how many languages they speak or what their family is like.

1 Choose someone in one of the pictures and write three questions you would like to ask them.

1 _____

2 _____

3 _____

2 A new child is about to join your class! You don't know anything about each other.

Draw a poster all about you and your background that you would like this new person to know.

3 A **refugee** is a person who has had to leave their home because of war, violence, conflict or persecution. They have moved to a new country to find safety and security. UNCRC Article 7 says that everyone has a right to a name and a land to call their own. If a child and their family have to leave their home quickly, they should be supported in finding a new home in a new country if they are not able to return.

What would you need to do to make a refugee feel welcome in your school?

_____
_____
_____
_____
_____
_____
_____
_____

What new things have you learned?

What had you not thought about before?

Human Rights

Rights defenders

> **Objective**
>
> **HR3.5D** – Be able to find out about examples in the local news of people who have defended the rights of others.

We will learn:

- to show appreciation for the work done by people to defend the rights of others
- how we can defend the rights of others.

Key vocabulary

defend, locality, rights

ⓘ Rights are worth defending! We can all be rights defenders by seeing where there are injustices and trying to do something about it. You may know people in your **locality** who are rights defenders.

1 a) What does it mean to '**defend**' someone? Tick **all** the correct answers.

☐ To protect someone from harm
☐ To take their side when they are in need of support
☐ To take someone's belongings
☐ To speak up for them when they need a friend
☐ To call someone names
☐ To upset someone

b) Choose a correct answer and draw a picture.

2 Create and decorate a poster showing your top tips for defending the **rights** of children in school.

For example:

If you see someone left out and ignored in the playground, start a new game and ask them to join in.

If you see someone being hurt, …

If you see someone calling someone a name, …

If you see someone not being listened to, …

What new things have you learned?

What had you not thought about before?

Good governance

Objective

PG3.6A – Be able to reflect on what makes a good leader and what makes a good team member.

We will learn:
- to recognise what makes a good team player
- to recognise what makes a good team leader
- how to be successful in each role.

Key vocabulary

abilities, leader, skills, team player

ⓘ When a group of people get together as a team, there are team members and one team leader. The team leader guides the team members. The whole team will have a range of **abilities** and skills between them. They should work together and, with the guidance of the team leader, they will have a good chance of reaching their goal. Are you a good team player?

Good governance: Session 1

1

a) Think of a time when you had to be a **team player**. This might have been when you played a sport, worked with others in your class or helped at home.
Draw what you did and add labels and captions.

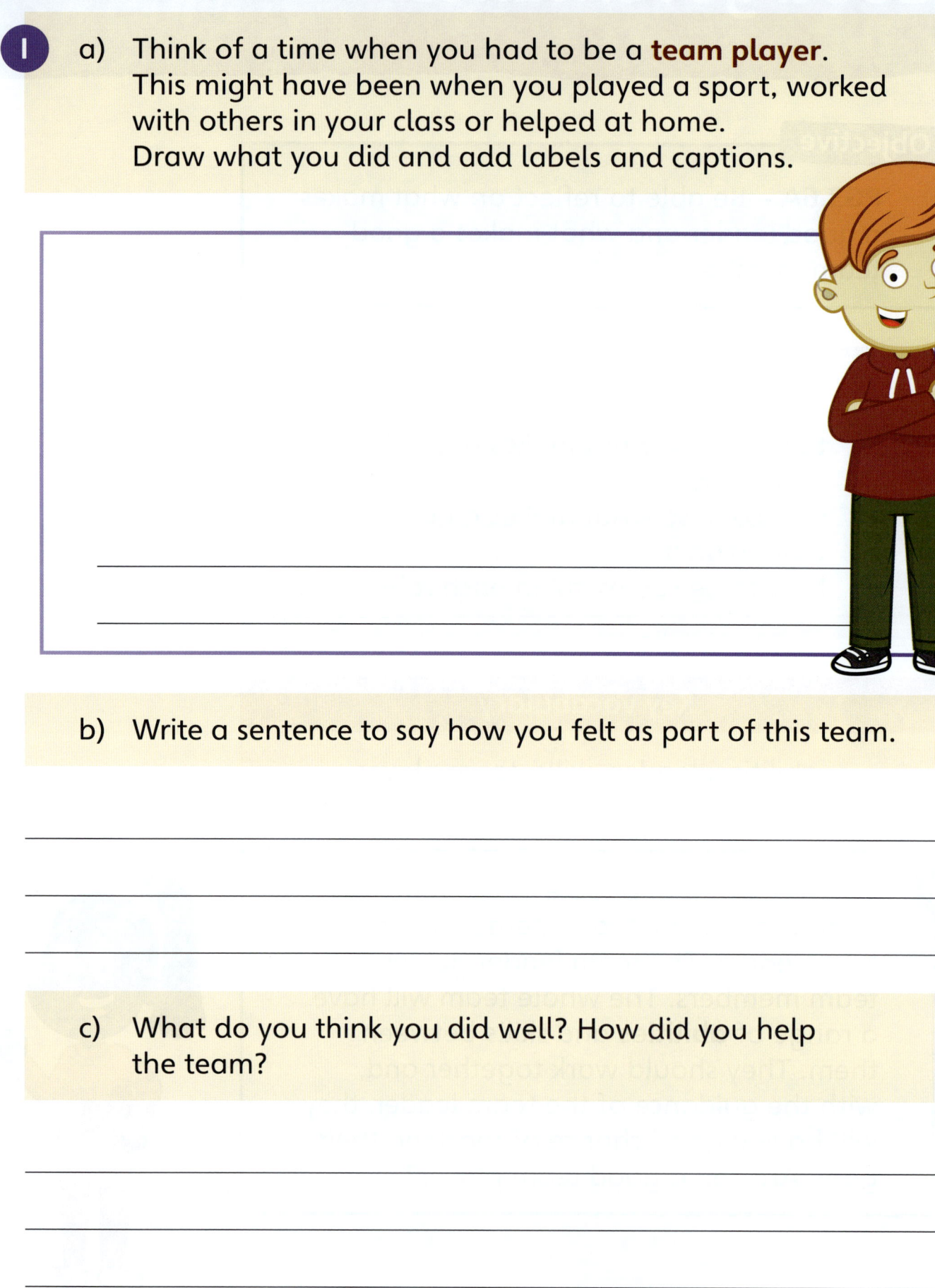

b) Write a sentence to say how you felt as part of this team.

_____

_____

c) What do you think you did well? How did you help the team?

_____

_____

Good governance: Session 1   119

2 Look at the **skills** you need to be a good team player or team **leader**. Draw a line to match the definitions with the words.

Definition	Word
Sharing your thoughts and ideas clearly with your team mates	reliable
Listening to the views of others and responding to them	tactical
Being honest so others know they can depend on you	trustworthy
Always behaving well so others have confidence in you	communicative
Planning well and planning in a clever way	good listener

3 Are there any other skills you can think of which are needed to be a successful team player or leader?

_____
_____
_____
_____

4 a) What skills do you have? Write a list of them.

_____
_____
_____

b) Write about a time when you used one of your strongest skills.

_____
_____
_____

c) Which skill from above do you think you need to work on to be a better team leader or team player?

_____
_____
_____

Good governance: Session 1   121

5 Do you know any leaders? For example, you may know the leader of your school, your country or your sports team. Make a list of leaders.

Leaders
• _____
• _____
• _____
• _____

6 Choose one leader you know about and draw them below. Label them with skills they have.

7 The skills needed by a team can change depending on what the team has to do. Look at these two teams.

Now look at the words. Which of these skills does the team leader of a team of doctors need? What skills would the ice hockey team leader need? Would they need any of the same skills? Write each skill in the table.

creative   trustworthy   positive attitude

intelligent   honest   good communicator

thoughtful   reliable   good listener

Team of doctors	Both	Ice hockey team

Good governance: Session 1   123

8 A local cricket team is looking for a new team member. Create a poster advertising this role. Make sure you include the skills needed in your advert!

What new things have you learned?

What had you not thought about before?

Power and Governance

Participation and inclusion

Objective

PG3.6B – Understand that the right to be listened to, and the willingness to listen to the viewpoint of others, is important in school and beyond.

We will learn:

- to recognise the importance of being listened to
- to recognise the importance of listening to others.

Key vocabulary

listening

ⓘ Have you ever talked to someone and realised they were not **listening**? How did it make you feel? We all have the right to be listened to. Equally, we must ensure that we listen to others, so that their ideas and opinions are heard.

Participation and inclusion: Session 2 125

1 What does it feel like to be ignored? What might happen if you try to speak to someone and they do not listen to you? Write an idea in each box.

_____

What it feels like to be ignored

_____

2 What does it feel like to be listened to? What could happen when someone listens carefully to someone else? Write an idea in each box.

_____

What it feels like to be listened to

_____

Participation and inclusion: Session 2

3 When you have something on your mind and it's bothering you, what do you do? Who do you tell?

When something is bothering me, I …

_____

_____

If I have a problem, I know I can talk to …

_____

_____

4 You are reading a book that's really exciting and you can't wait to get to the end. Just as you're nearly finished, your friend Alexa comes over. She wants to talk to you about her parents and how they are arguing a lot at the moment. She looks very sad. What should you do?

_____

_____

_____

_____

What new things have you learned?

What had you not thought about before?

Glossary

abilities – someone's level of skill at doing something

affect – to do something that produces an effect or change in something or in someone's situation

assumptions – things you think are true although you have no definite proof

bullying – someone who uses their strength or power to frighten or hurt someone who is weaker

carnivore – an animal that feeds on other animals

climate – the typical weather conditions in a particular area or over time

collaboratively – working together with another person or group to achieve something

compromising – to reach an agreement in which everyone involved accepts less than what they wanted at first

conflict – a state of disagreement or argument between people, groups and countries

connections – the way in which two facts, ideas or events are related to each other; a sense of sharing something with another person

consequence – something that happens as a result of a particular action or set of conditions

consumer – someone who buys and uses products and services

currency – the system or type of money that a country uses

defend – to do something in order to protect someone or something from being attacked

differences – ways in which two or more people or things are not like each other

disability – a physical or mental condition that makes it harder for someone to use a part of their body, or to learn

discrimination – the practice of treating one person or group differently from another in an unfair way

effect – a change that is caused by an event and/or action

entitled – someone that has the official or perceived right to have or do something

Glossary

equality – a situation in which people have the same rights and advantages

expensive – costing a lot of money

expertise – special skills or knowledge in a particular subject, that you learn by experience or training

fact – a piece of information that is known to be true

fairly – treating everyone in a way that is right or equal

food chain – all animals and plants considered as a group in which a plant is eaten by an insect or animal, which is then eaten by another animal

fossil fuels – a fuel such as coal or oil, produced by the gradual decaying of plants and animals

generalisation – a statement about all the members of a group that may be true in some or many situations but is not true in every case

generations – all people of about the same age

global issue – an issue that affects the entire world

habitat – the natural home of a plant or animal

herbivore – an animal that only eats plants

injustice – a situation in which people are treated very unfairly and not given their rights

interconnected – if two facts, ideas or events are interconnected, or if they interconnect, they are related and one is affected by or caused by the other

interest – if you have an interest in something or someone, you want to know or learn more about them

judgements – an opinion that you form, especially after thinking carefully about something

justice – fairness in the way people are treated

landfill – a place where waste is buried under the ground

leader – the person who directs or controls a group, organisation or country

listening – to pay attention to what someone is saying or to a sound that you can hear

Glossary

local – relating to the particular area you live in, or the area you are talking about

locality – a small area of a country or a city

mental well-being – the feeling of being well in one's mind, being able to cope with daily life and experiences

necessity – something that you need to have in order to live

need – a situation in which something is necessary, especially something that is not happening yet or is not yet available

omnivore – an animal that eats both meat and plants

opinion – your ideas or beliefs about a particular subject

opportunity – a chance to do something or an occasion when it is possible to do something

outdoors – outside, not in a building

peace – a situation in which there is no war or fighting

prejudice – an unreasonable dislike and distrust of people who are different from you in some way, especially because of their race, sex or religion

prey – an animal or bird that is hunted and eaten by another animal

produced – to make or write something to be bought, used or enjoyed by people

recycle – the reprocessing of used objects or materials so that they can be used again

reduce – to make something smaller or less in size, amount or price

refugee – someone who has been forced to leave their country, especially during a war, or for political or religious reasons

refuse – to say firmly that you will not do something that someone has asked you to do

remodel – to change the shape, structure or appearance of something, especially a building

repair – to fix something that is damaged, broken, split or not working properly

resolve – to find a satisfactory way of dealing with a problem or difficulty

response – something that is done as a reaction to something that has happened or been said

Glossary

responsible – having a duty to be in charge of or to look after someone or something

reuse – to use something again

rights – something that you are allowed to do or have

self-esteem – the feeling of being content with who you are

similarities – if there are similarities between two things or people, they share similar features

skills – abilities to do something well, especially because you have learned and practised it

solution – a way of solving a problem or dealing with a difficult situation

source – a thing, place or activity that you get something from; the cause of something, especially a problem, or the place where it starts

space – the amount of an area, room or container that is empty or available to be used

stereotype – a belief or idea of what a particular type of person or thing is like. Stereotypes are often unfair or untrue

support – to help someone by being sympathetic and kind to them

sustainability – able to continue without causing damage to the environment

synonym – a word with the same meaning as another word in the same language

team player – someone who works well as a member of a team, especially in business

unfairly – in a manner that is not right or fair, especially because not everyone has an equal opportunity

unfairness – not treating everyone equally

United Nations Convention of the Rights of the Child (UNCRC) – a legally-binding international agreement setting out the civil, political, economic, social and cultural rights of every child, regardless of their race, religion or abilities

United Nations Goodwill Ambassador – distinguished individuals that help focus global attention on the work of the United Nations, appointed by the heads of the United

Nations Funds, Programmes and specialised agencies

United Nations Messenger of Peace – distinguished individuals that help focus global attention on the work of the United Nations, appointed by the Secretary-General of the UN

unique – of which only one or very few exists; something that is rare

value – the importance or usefulness of something

want – to have a desire for something

wealthy – material wealth: having a lot of money or possessions; emotional wealth: having support from family and friends, feeling valued